Quiet Coloring

A coloring book
for stopping the noise
and finding self kindness

Judith T. Krauthamer

Quiet Coloring. A coloring book for stopping the noise and finding self kindness

Published by Chalcedony Press, Ellicott City, Maryland. U.S.A.

Book Cover and Graphics by Judith T. Krauthamer

ISBN: 978-0-9895035-2-5

For correspondences:
2017 website: www.quietspacecoaching.com

INTRODUCTION

There are four things philosophers and wisdom teachers believe to be true

All human beings suffer even though it may not appear so.

All human beings are connected, despite feeling separate or alone.

The thoughts and stories human beings create feel real—and are not true.

All human beings are worthy of a life of joy.

There is one thing I think to be true

There are many of us who have a hard time believing any one of those four.

There is one thing I know to be true

This coloring book will help those of us who are disbelievers.

Coloring provides a brief respite, a vacation, from the world within us and the world around us. Whether we are stressed or simply in need of creating art, time spent coloring is our oasis. It is a meditative art form. The act of coloring, picking up our pens and pencils, gently removes us from our daily lives.

Coloring is a wonderful way to find quiet for those of us who are easily triggered or dismayed. We belong to a group of people who are "neuro-atypical."

Those of us who are neuro-atypical represent at least 20%, or one fifth of the world's population. That means in a class or at a party where there are ten people, at least two of them have a brain that is not typical. Our brains are wired differently. Not better or worse-- simply different.

We live perfectly normal lives, except that we can be easily thrown off by visual or auditory triggers. We might have intrusive thoughts or feelings that seem to have a life of their own. We may have difficulty focusing on specific tasks or may have the need to take many breaks while working or studying. For some of us, our challenges have diagnostic names, such as obsessive compulsive disorder

(OCD), attention deficit disorder (ADD), or misophonia (a rage reaction to auditory triggers, most commonly chewing sounds).

Quiet Coloring. A coloring book for stopping the noise and finding self kindness.

Quiet Coloring is the perfect art book for us. In addition to the calming effect of simply coloring, the graphics are specifically crafted to shift our thoughts and our feelings. Quiet Coloring is modeled after cognitive behavior therapy, a therapy that seeks to change thought patterns by presenting new ways of thinking. The pictures reinforce that we are not alone in our suffering. There are messages to remind us to breathe deeply, which helps us to focus and ease our bodies.

The graphics present the idea that we can give ourselves permission to let go of thoughts and worry. By coloring the statements, such as "I am more than my thoughts," we physically take in, or embody, the self-care messages. In the time it takes to complete a coloring page, we validate our worth.

I hope that you find the coloring relaxing and meaningful.

Have fun and enjoy!

In partnership,

Judith T. Krauthamer, M.S.

Founder, Quietspace Coaching

Author, "Sound-Rage. A primer of the neurobiology and psychology of a little known anger disorder."

My thoughts are just stories.
They feel real, but they are not true.

What matters is the here and now.

I give myself
permission
to experience
joy

For right now, I
will only think
about today.

I let my thoughts
come and then fly away.
I am more than
my thoughts.

Today I practice deep breathing.

Breathe in for 4 seconds.

Hold for 4 seconds.

Breathe out for 4 seconds.

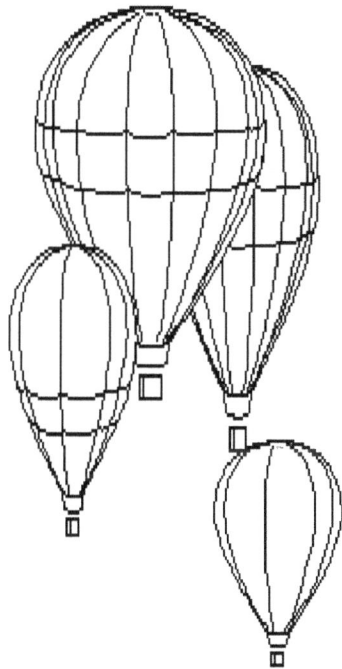

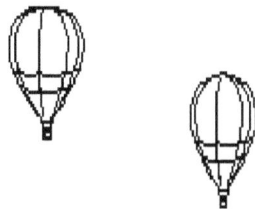

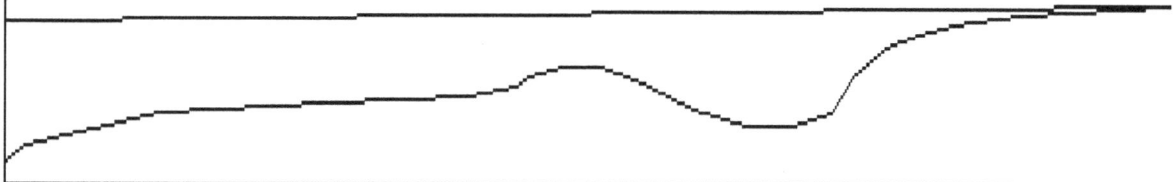

I quiet my anger.
No one is trying to hurt me.

3 things
that bring me joy:

_____

_____

_____

I breathe
calmly
and
slowly

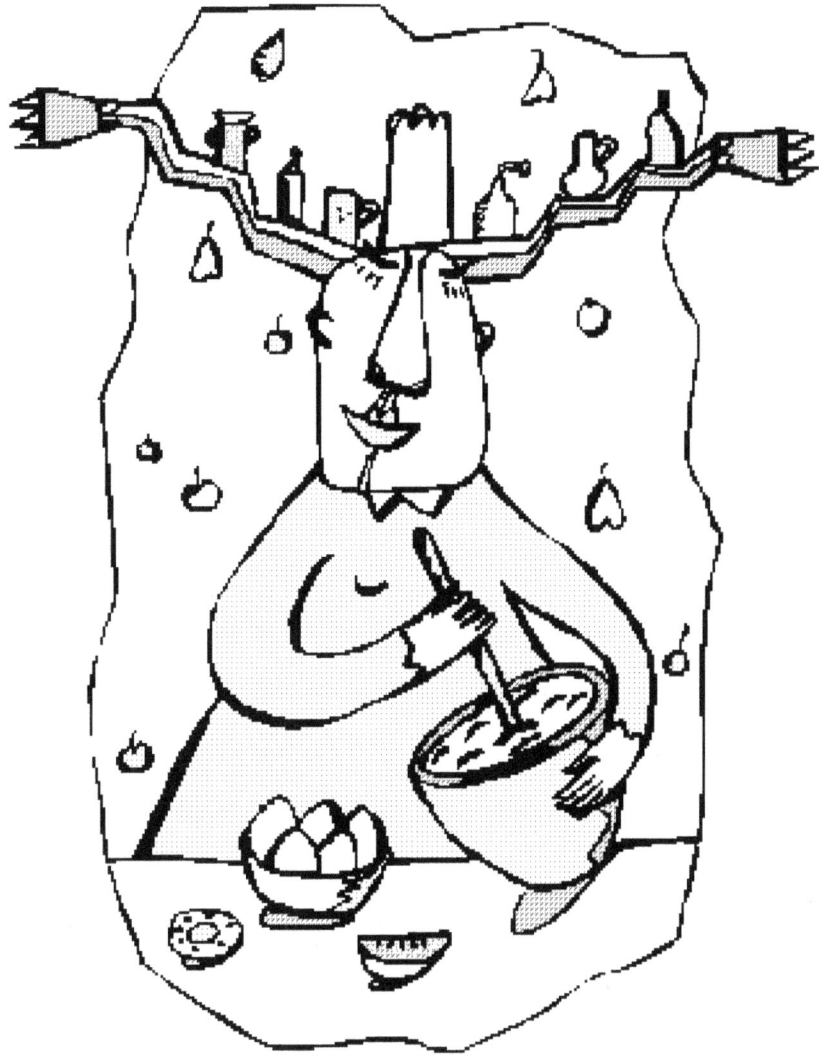

I will practice
self-compassion

I observe my thoughts.
Instead of judging them
or myself
I think, "How interesting."

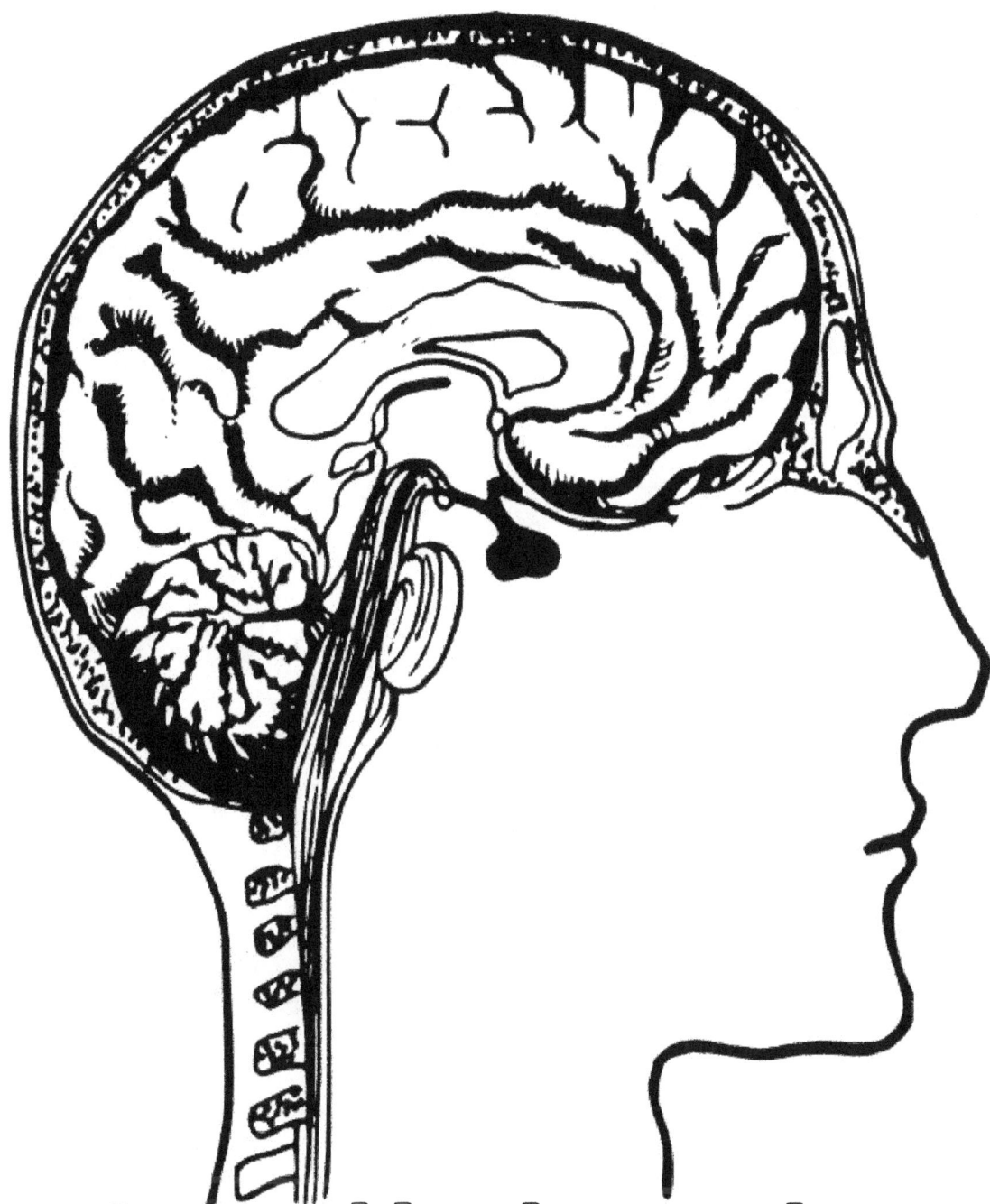

I talk back
to the voice
that tells me
I am powerless

I practice
breathing
slowly
and deeply

Today I will be worry-free

for two minutes.

I forgive myself.
I forgive others.

Bad Days
Are Inevitable

There is no shame in being different.

In fact, it is a gift to be unique.

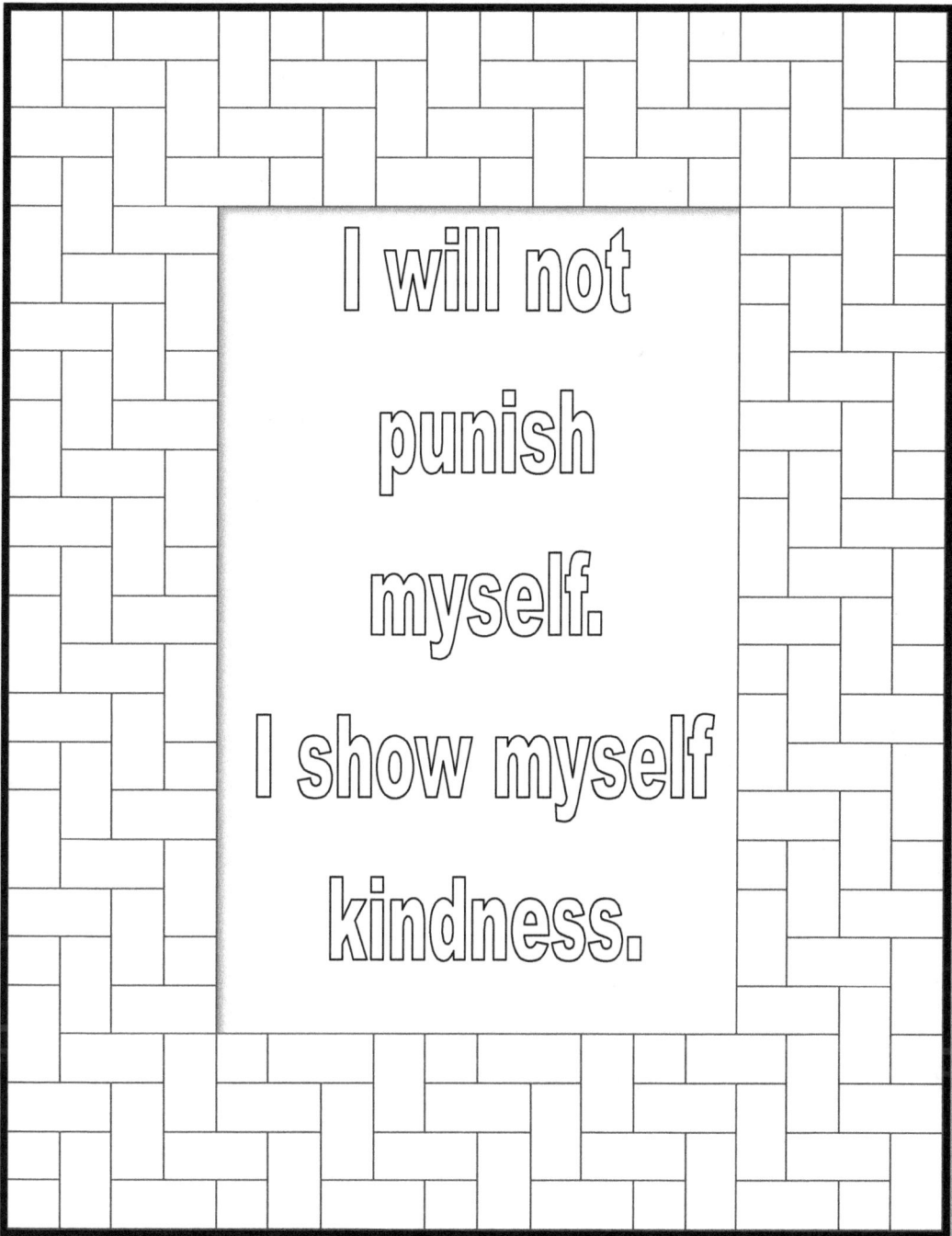

I will not

punish

myself.

I show myself

kindness.

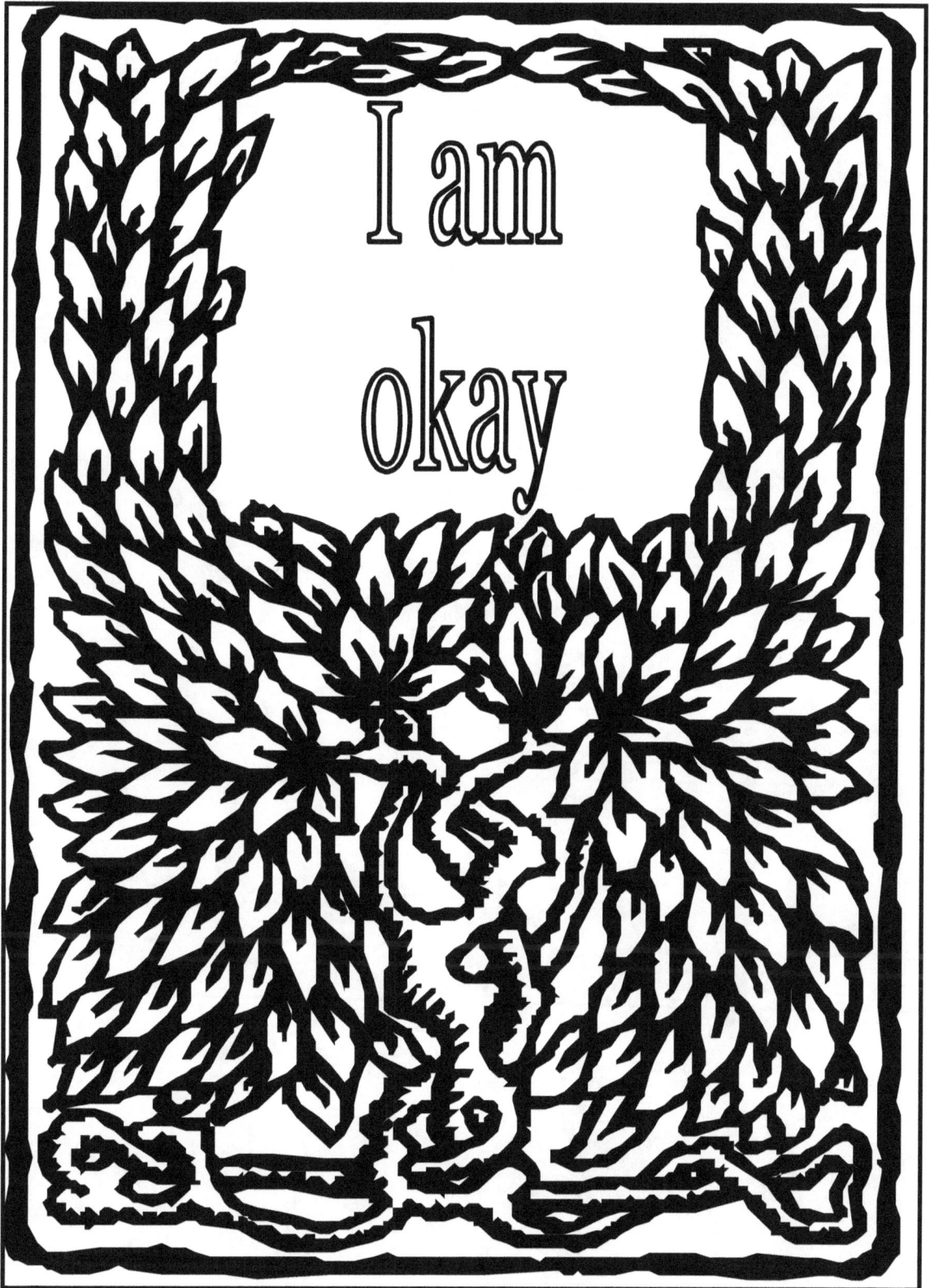

I am

okay

I will be patient with myself

I observe
my rituals
without judgment

Everyone Needs to be Heard

I focus on my breathing.

My real self

is bigger

than my mind.

Most people believe
they see the world as it is.
However,

We really see the world
as we are.

"Your worst enemy
can not harm you
as much as your
own unguarded thoughts."
Buddha

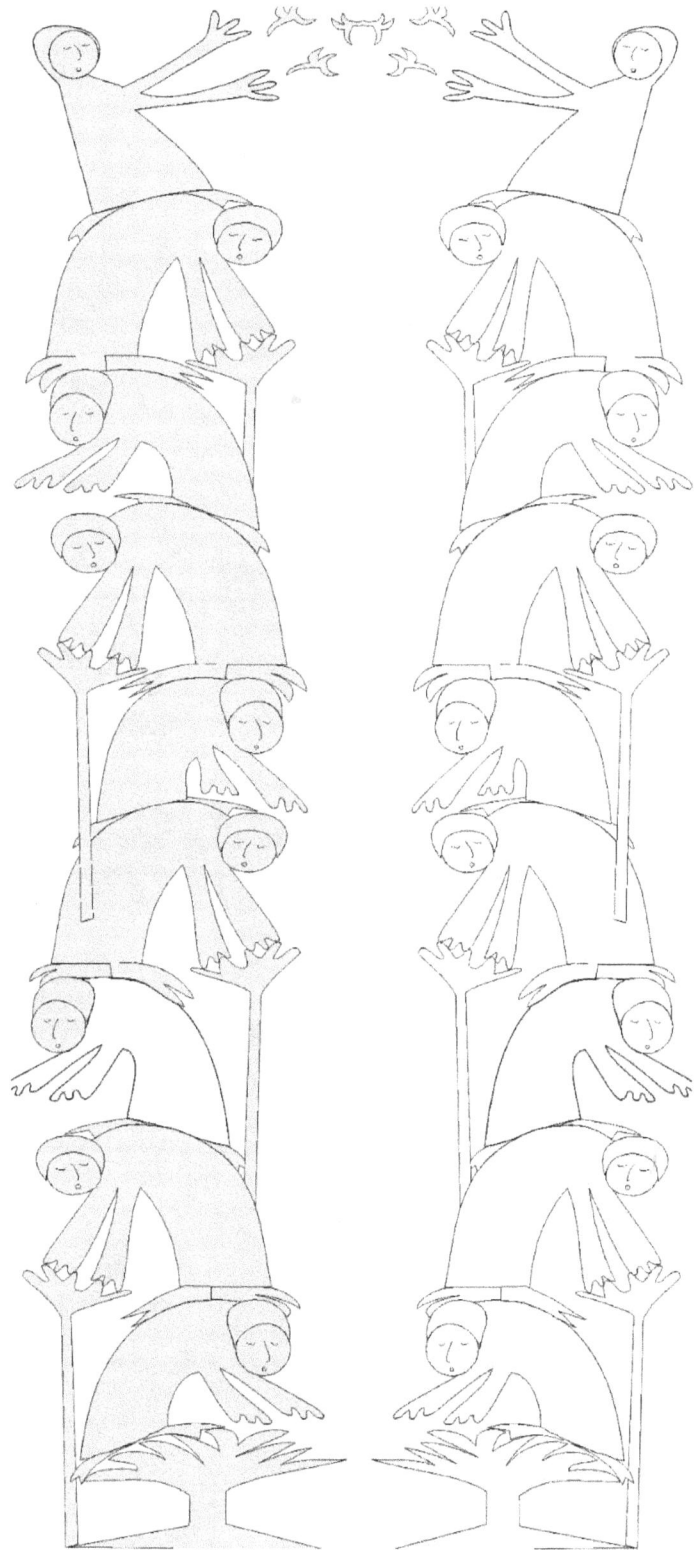

I will ask for help when I need help

I am bigger
than my thoughts

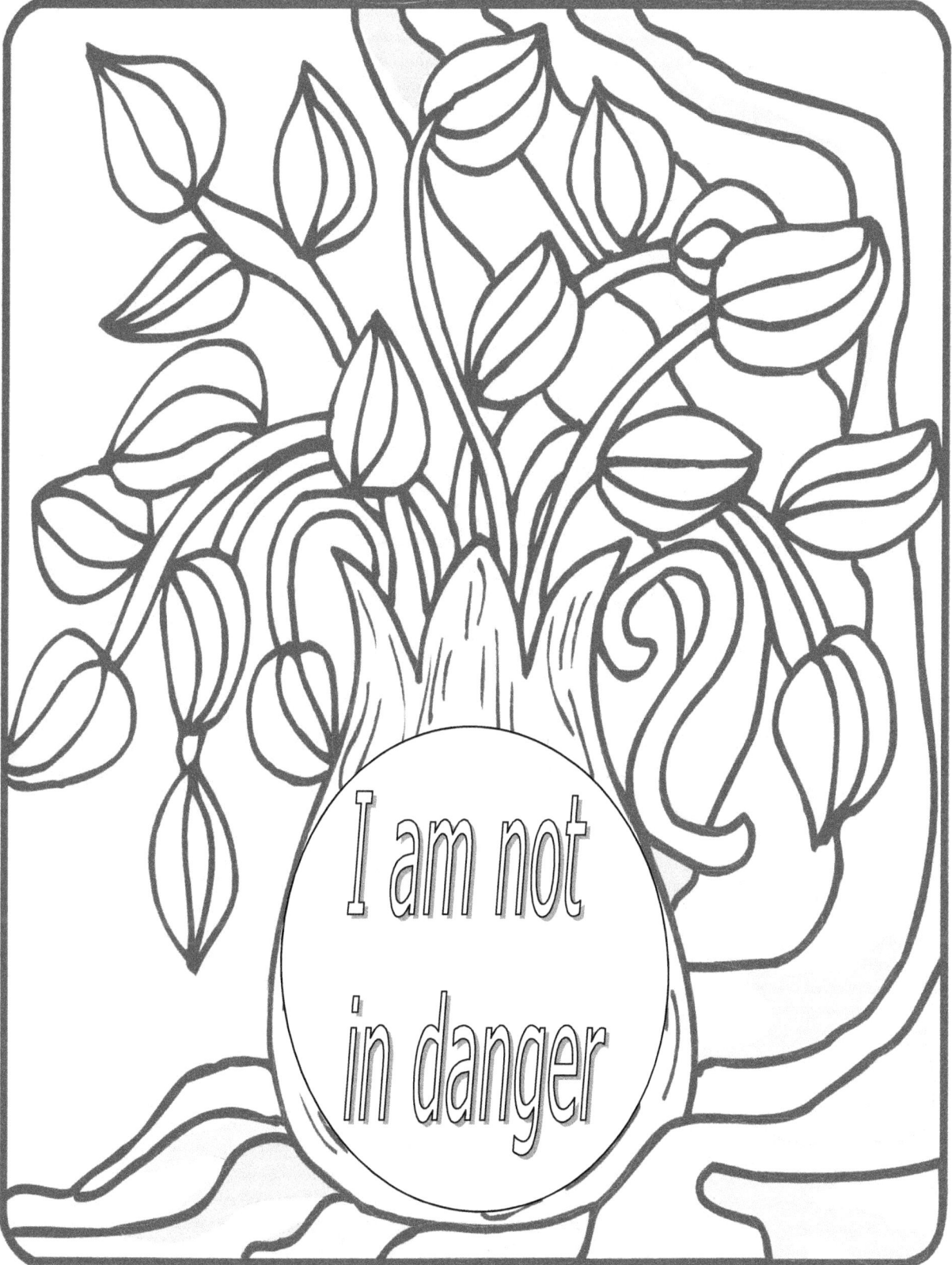

I am not
in danger

I can
manage
my
anger

I am safe

I allow myself
to feel sad.

My anger
is from my brain.
I use empathy
to quiet it.

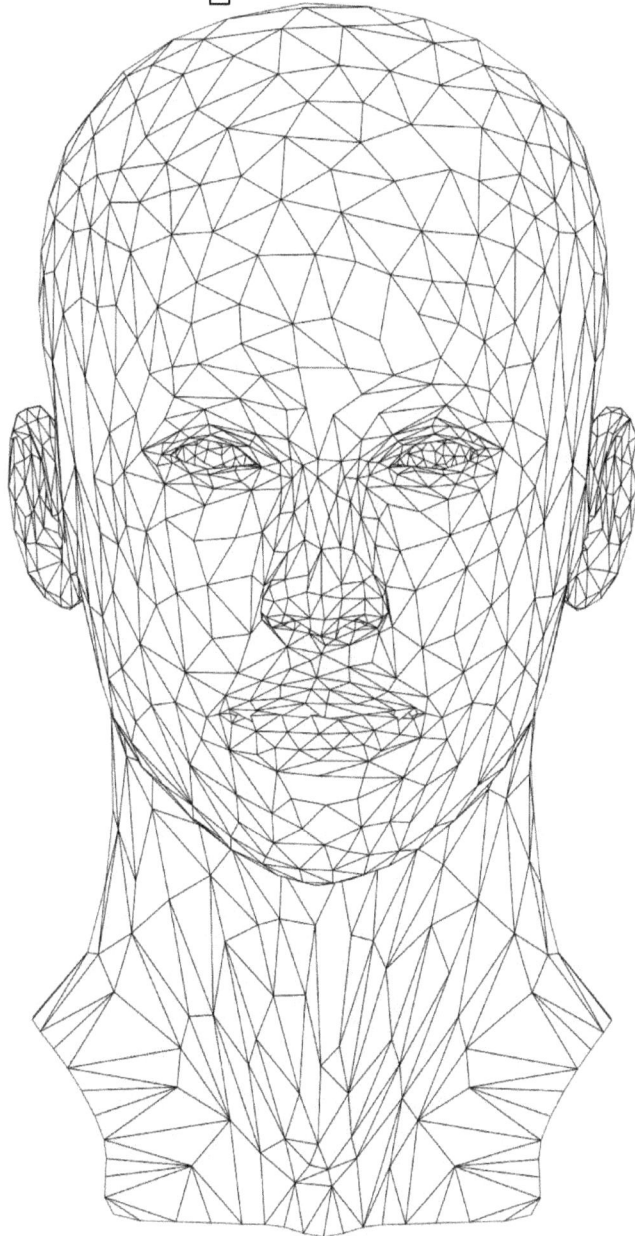

Sadness is part of the human condition.

Everyone
has a need
to be loved.

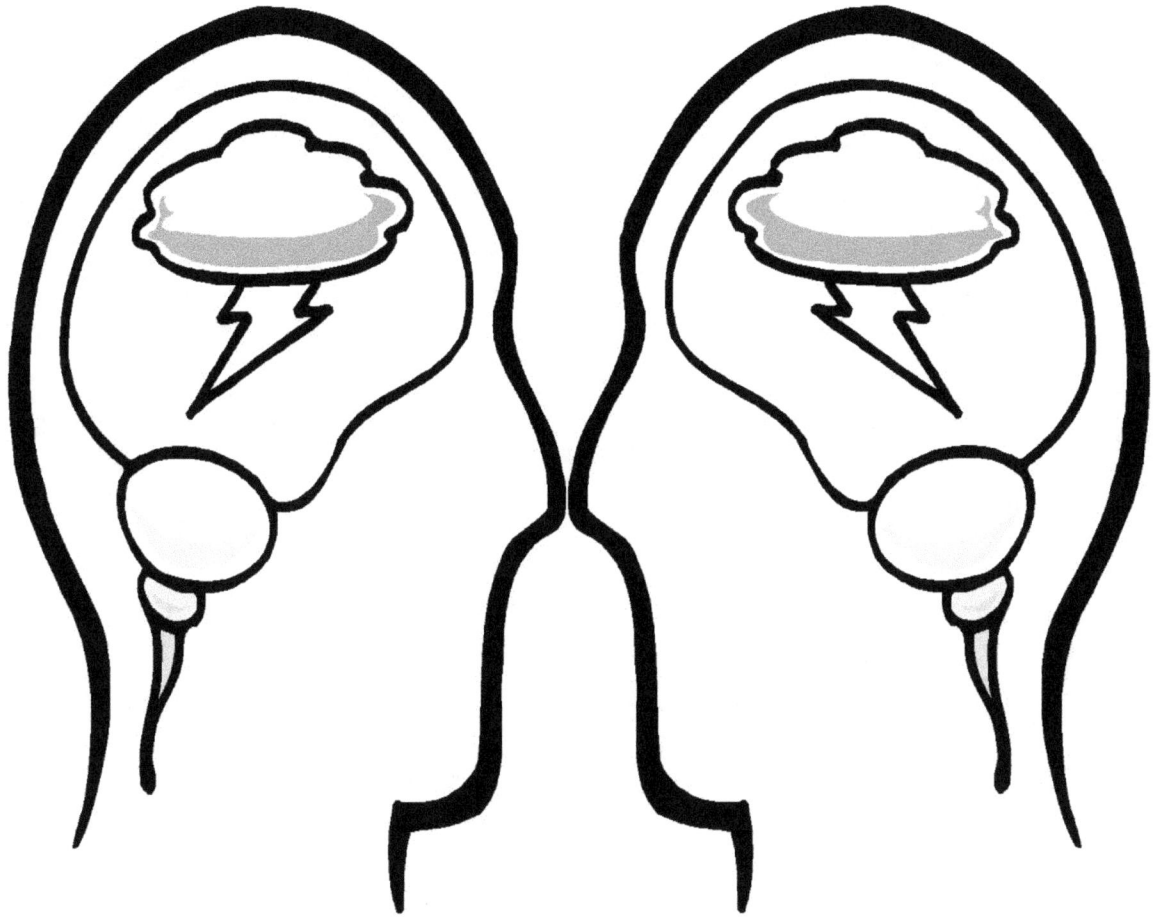

When I feel hatred

I say to myself,

"I choose love."

I let go
of shame

I acknowledge my disorder
and I know
I am much more
than my disorder.

Things will

and do

get better.

I may feel alone.
In reality,
I am not alone.
All human beings
are connected.

Facing fears
makes them shrink.

I am worthy
of a life of joy

All Human Beings

Struggle

Noises may anger me
but they can not
harm me

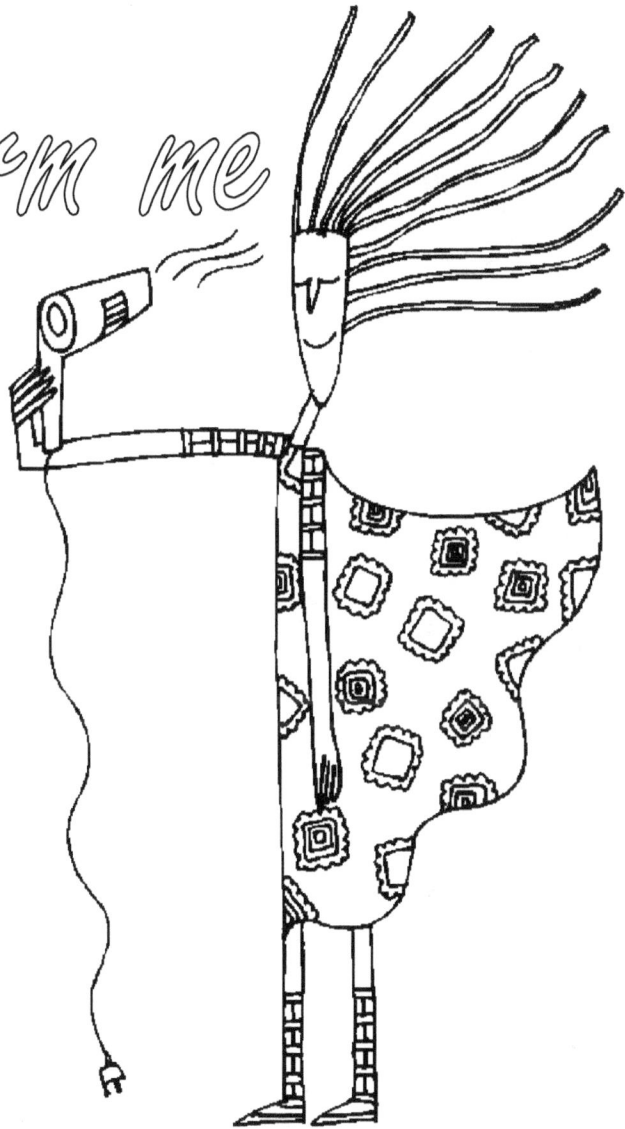

www.ingramcontent.com/pod-product-compliance
Lightning Source LLC
Chambersburg PA
CBHW081650270326
41933CB00018B/3410

* 9 7 8 0 9 8 9 5 0 3 5 2 5 *